MW01172240

First printing 2016, Copyright ᴢ0ₐᴐ, ₙₑ...

Actual Bible quotes are followed by the Bible version quoted:

(NASB) (NKJV) (NIV)

Scripture addresses otherwise are listed to reference for study.

To obtain copies of this book:

Updated February 1, 2023

This paperback book is currently available to order online.

Go to "Amazon."

Type in "books" then type in full title:

"You can know that you are saved your salvation in Christ"

Author: Mary Ann Francis

<u>This is the book</u>
<u>that I wish</u>

<u>someone would have given to me</u>.

Simple understanding but if any of the pieces

are missing – we can stumble with uncertainty.

<u>The center of this book opens to Scripture</u>

<u>and a prayer of salvation</u>. (p. 28-29)

It can be prayed at any time,

even before this book is read.

We need only to believe in Jesus and call on Him.

Not even a prayer is needed – but a prayer is simply

talking with God and it helps most feel resolved and

affirmed in their decision to surrender themselves

to receive a righteousness from God that is not of

ourselves but through what Christ has done for us.

To make that connection with Him is to remain

with Him and walk with Him – to belong to Him.

Christianity is not a religion; it is a relationship with

God in which our spirit is joined with His Spirit.

<u>I Corinthians 6:17</u> (NASB)

But the one who joins himself to the Lord

is one spirit with Him.

Table of Contents:

Christianity is <u>not</u> about behavior management.

It is about <u>the transformation</u> that occurs <u>in us</u> as we

understand <u>God's love</u> for us and <u>our value</u> to Him -

the value of <u>the ransom</u> He gave

<u>to reconcile us to Himself forever</u>.

Our Position in Christ

Jesus died for all our sins before we had

yet committed any of them.

Hebrews 10:10-12

Everyone who believes in Him

receives forgiveness.

Acts 10:43

In Christ Jesus, we are righteous.

II Corinthians 5:21

He seated us with Him in the heavenly places.

Ephesians 2:6

He who believes in Jesus is one spirit with Him.

I Corinthians 6:17

God created Adam and Eve for fellowship with Him.

Adam and Eve walked and talked with God. - Genesis 3:8-11

They had children, who also had children...

now there are 7-8 billion people on the earth. But we are

not alive because our parents had children. We live -

because God created each of us for fellowship with Him.

<u>God</u>

<u>Created</u>

<u>You</u>

God does not have human limitations -

God's love is not divided among us.

His love is complete and total for each of us.

God created each of us in His own image to belong to Him.

In His own image

Genesis 1:27 (NASB)

God created man in His own image,
in the image of God He created him;
male and female He created them.

Genesis 2:7 (NASB)

Then the Lord God formed man of dust of the ground,
and breathed into his nostrils the breath of life;
and man became a living being.

Psalm 139:13-14 (NASB)

For You formed my inward parts;
You wove me in my mother's womb.
I will give thanks to You, for
I am fearfully and wonderfully made;
Wonderful are Your works,
And my soul knows it very well.

Isaiah 42:5 (NASB)

Thus says God the Lord,
Who created the heavens and stretched them out,
Who spread out the earth and its offspring,
Who gives breath to the people on it
And spirit to those who walk in it,

God created us because He wants us

He brought us into existence through an act of His will.

He created us for the purpose of fellowship with Him.

He refers to anyone who believes in His Son as <u>His child</u>.

He refers to the church as <u>His bride</u>.

He refers to Abraham as <u>His friend</u>.

These are the closest relationships that we have.

<u>We are all of these to Him when we receive</u>

<u>His great gift of salvation</u>.

Sin separated us from God, but He had a plan.

The price He paid to redeem us was His only begotten Son.

<u>He desires that everyone be saved</u>. - I Timothy 2:3-4

His salvation is offered to everyone. - I John 2:2

<u>Christ gave Himself as a ransom for all</u>.

<u>Jesus died in our place</u>.

He received the punishment that we could never bear.

He rose from the dead as our justification.

He sent us the Holy Spirit.

We receive the Holy Spirit once we believe in Christ.

He seats us with Him in the heavenly places.

<u>God's love for us is unsearchable</u>.

<u>Our value to Him is unequaled</u>.

We are not judged who believe in Christ.
John 3:18, 5:24

He has made us righteous - His Spirit dwells in us.

His Spirit will never leave us nor forsake us. - Hebrews 13:5

His Spirit convicts us of our righteousness. - John 16:10

Our life is transformed by the revealing of Christ in us.

Our self-image changes as we realize our value to Him.

As we receive His love, we are able to love ourselves.

We can then love others as well as ourselves. - Mark 12:31

Love does no wrong. - Romans 13:10

Perfect love casts out all fear - I John 4:17-18

when we know that we are accepted by God.

Our punishment has been paid.

Our love is perfected in this confidence.

When He appears, He will receive us to Himself.

We will not shrink back at His coming but look forward to

the day that He will return for us. - John 14:3, Hebrews 9:28, 10:37-39

We have peace with God. - Romans 5:1

He has a plan for our lives here on earth,

but this is not our home. - Philippians 3:20, Hebrews 13:14

Jesus is the fulfillment of the law. - Matthew 5:17, Romans 8:3-4

He puts His law on our hearts and minds. - Hebrews 10:16

He is our God and we are His people. - Hebrews 8:10

As He is so are we in this world. - I John 4:17

God's plan for each of us is salvation – but we must receive it.
God used a man, who had once been foremost of all sinners,
to write a large portion of the New Testament of the Bible.
His name was Saul who would later be known as Paul.
God did this as a display of His patience toward us so that -
all would know that they too could be saved. - I Timothy 1:15-16

God

Wants

You

Some are intimidated to think they could never live a Christian life -
without Him, we cannot. When we believe in Jesus as our Savior,
the Holy Spirit comes to live in us and guides us to follow our Lord.
We are transformed only through this very fellowship with Jesus.

He wants all saved

I Timothy 2:3-4 (NKJV)

For this is good and acceptable in the sight of

God our Savior, who desires all men to be saved

and to come to the knowledge of the truth.

For there is one God and one Mediator

between God and men, the Man Christ Jesus,

who gave Himself as a ransom for all,

to be testified in due time,

II Peter 3:9 (NASB)

The Lord is not slow about His promise,

as some count slowness, but is patient toward you,

not wishing for any to perish

but for all to come to repentance.

Acts 2:21 (NASB)

'And it shall be that everyone who

calls on the name of the Lord will be saved.'

Jesus came from heaven to give -----

Matthew 1:23 (NKJV)

"Behold the virgin shall be with child, and bear a Son,

and they shall call His name Immanuel,"

which is translated, "God with us." - Isaiah 7:14

A woman named Mary was engaged to a man named Joseph.

An angel appeared to her and told her she was favored of God.

Mary agreed to be the mother of Jesus. - Luke 1:38

The Holy Spirit overshadowed her. - Luke 1:35

She became pregnant with the Son of God. - Luke 1:35, Micah 5:2

Joseph kept her a virgin until Jesus was born. - Matthew 1:25

Jesus lived a sinless life. - II Corinthians 5:21

He did not have the bloodline of fallen mankind.

God is His Father - He inherited His bloodline from His Father.

This is the perfect blood shed to pay the price for our sins.

Jesus calls God His Father. - Luke 2:49, John 5:18, 6:32-33, 6:40, 8:54

God calls Jesus His Son. - Matthew 3:17, 17:5, Mark 1:11, Luke 3:22, 9:35

God made man in His own image. God then came as a man

to put away our sins. - Colossians 2:9, Hebrews 9:26, Philippians 2:6-11

Jesus is one with the Father. - John 10:30 - He came from heaven.

Jesus left heaven and became a man to overcome sin. - John 16:28

Jesus returned to heaven and intercedes for us. - Hebrews 7:24-28

Jesus was conceived of the Holy Spirit. - Matthew 1:20, Luke 1:34-35

He came from heaven to save us from our sins. - Matthew 1:21

-----His life in exchange for us

Jesus was without sin, yet He was baptized. - Matthew 3:13-17

He said so that all righteousness would be fulfilled.

He did this out of love for us so that we would do the same.

His Heavenly Father affirmed Him. Heaven was opened.

The Spirit descended upon Him - Luke 3:21-22, Mark 1:9-11

... and remained. - John 1:32-33

He healed all who came to Him. He forgave sin. - Luke 5:20-25

He told us of His Father, Who can be our Father. - John 20:17

He fulfilled all that had been prophesied of His life.

He cast out demons, cleansed lepers and raised the dead.

Jesus came to rescue us and redeem us to Himself. - Titus 2:14

Jesus is the unblemished and spotless sacrifice. - I Peter 1:18-19

When John the Baptist saw Him, he said, - John 1:29

"Behold the Lamb of God
who takes away the sin of the world!"

Jesus was the final sacrifice for all mankind for all time.

He said, "No one takes My life from Me. I lay it down."

Also, "For this reason I came, to do thy will O Father."

Galatians 2:20 (NASB)

...the Son of God, who loved me and

and gave Himself up for me.

Jesus was crucified, died and was buried. - I Corinthians 15:3-4

On the third day, He was resurrected from the dead.

Death could not hold Him because He was without sin.

If we receive Jesus, His Spirit in us will also resurrect us.

Shadow of the Savior

A Passover Lamb

was slain each year for each household.

But the prophets foretold of

The Lamb of God who would come.

Exodus 12, Isaiah 53, Hebrews 9:12, 22, 26

Without the shedding of blood, there is no remission of sins.

Before the final sacrifice of Christ being crucified,

a person would bring a lamb to be sacrificed.

The priest looked at the lamb: it had to be without blemish.

He did not look at the person presenting the lamb.

He understood the person had sin to be forgiven.

The person placed their hand onto the lamb.

The person's sins were transferred to the lamb.

The lamb was slain.

The person left with their sins covered

for another year.

Jesus is the Savior

Jesus is our Passover

He is the final sacrifice - it is finished.

When John the Baptist saw Jesus, He said,

"Behold the Lamb of God."

John 1:29, Matthew 26:2, I Corinthians 5:7

Where there is forgiveness of these things,

There are no longer sacrifices for sin. - Hebrews 10:17-18

Jesus was the final sacrifice. - Hebrews 10-10-12

Christ Jesus is the Passover. He is without sin.

He does not reject us because of our sins.

He came to save sinners.

We receive Christ by placing our faith in Him.

Jesus bore all our sins on the cross.

He was crucified as a ransom for us.

In Him, our sins are removed

Forever...

If we seek to establish a righteousness of our own,

we fail to subject ourselves to the righteousness of God:

We subject ourselves to the righteousness of God by faith in what

Jesus has done for us, through the sacrifice of Himself on the cross.

If we walk by the Spirit, we do not carry out the desires of the flesh.

To walk by the leading of the Holy Spirit in us is to walk with God.

Romans 10:3-4, Philippians 3:9, Galatians 5:16, II Corinthians 5:21

God

Justified

You

We are self-righteous if we think we do not need a Savior -

no-one is without sin. Our God is a perfect and Holy God.

We are self-righteous if we think we are too bad to be saved -

we are not believing that Jesus is a sufficient sacrifice.

Jesus took our sins

Romans 3:23-24 (NASB)

for all have sinned and fall short of the glory of God,

being justified as a gift by His grace

through the redemption which is in Christ Jesus;

II Corinthians 5:21 (NKJV)

For He made Him who knew no sin to be sin for us, that

we might become the righteousness of God in Him.

Romans 4:25 (NASB)

He who was delivered over because of our transgressions,

and was raised because of our justification.

Hebrews 10:10-12 (NASB)

By this will we have been sanctified through

the offering of the body of Jesus Christ once for all.

Every priest stands daily ministering and offering

time after time the same sacrifices, which can never

take away sins; but He, having offered one sacrifice

for sins for all time, sat down at the right hand of God,

Jesus came to save the whole world

His salvation is offered to everyone.

Acts 2:21, I John 2:2, 4:14, Revelation 7:9

John 3:16-18 (NKJV)

"For God so loved the world that He gave

His only begotten Son, that whoever believes in Him

should not perish but have everlasting life.

"For God did not send His Son into the world to condemn

the world, but that the world through Him might be saved.

"He who believes in Him is not condemned; but he

who does not believe is condemned already, because

he has not believed in the name of the only begotten Son of God.

John 5:24 (NKJV)

"Most assuredly, I say to you, he who hears My word

and believes in Him who sent Me has everlasting life,

and shall not come into judgement,

but has passed from death into life.

Jesus said the word He spoke is what will condemn us,

if He is rejected by us in unbelief. – John 12:48

Everyone who believes (sheep) receives forgiveness of sins.

Only those who reject Him (goats) will remain condemned.

Only His righteousness makes us acceptable. – Romans 10:3-4

Our self-righteousness is not acceptable for salvation.

All judgement has been given to the Son, because He is the Son of man. - John 5:27

John 5:22-23 (NIV)

Moreover, the Father judges no one, but

has entrusted all judgement to the Son, that all

may honor the Son just as they honor the Father.

He who does not honor the Son

does not honor the Father, who sent him.

Revelation 6:16-17 (NASB)

and they said to the mountains and the rocks,

"Fall on us and hide us from

the presence of Him who sits on the throne,

and from the wrath of the Lamb;

for the great day of their wrath has come,

and who is able to stand?"

Jesus said His sheep hear His voice and He knows them. They follow Him. - John 10:27

Matthew 25:31-32 (NKJV)

"When the Son of Man comes in His glory, and

all the holy angels with Him, then He will sit on the

throne of His glory. "All the nations will be gathered

before Him, and He will separate them from one another,

as a shepherd divides the sheep from the goats.

You are redeemed

I Peter 2:24-25 (NASB)

and He Himself bore our sins in His body on the cross,

so that we might die to sin and live to righteousness;

for by His wounds you were healed.

For you were continually straying like sheep,

but now you have returned to the

Shepherd and Guardian of your souls.

Titus 2:14 (NASB)

who gave Himself for us

to redeem us from every lawless deed, and to

purify for Himself a people for His own possession,

zealous for good deeds.

Titus 3:4-6 (NKJV)

But when the kindness and the love

of God our Savior toward man appeared,

not by works of righteousness which we have done,

but according to His mercy

He saved us,

through the washing of regeneration

and renewing of the Holy Spirit,

whom He poured out on us abundantly

through Jesus Christ our Savior,

The blood of Christ

I Peter 1:18-19 (NIV)

For you know that it was not with

perishable things such as silver or gold that

you were redeemed from the empty way of life

handed down to you from your forefathers, but

with the precious blood of Christ,

a lamb without blemish or defect.

Hebrews 10:17-18 (NIV)

Then he adds: "Their sins and lawless acts

I will remember no more."

And where these have been forgiven,

there is no longer any sacrifice for sin.

Hebrews 9:26 (NASB)

Otherwise, He would have needed to suffer often

since the foundation of the world; but now once at

the consummation of the ages He has been manifested

to put away sin by the sacrifice of Himself.

Hebrews 9:14 (NASB)

how much more will the blood of Christ,

who through the eternal Spirit offered Himself

without blemish to God, cleanse your conscience

from dead works to serve the living God?

God is Love – He created us to be the recipient of His love.

God does not love anyone partially. His love is infinite.

His love is perfect and complete. Once we believe in Him,

Christ dwells in our hearts through faith - Ephesians 3:17-19

We become rooted and grounded in His love.

His Spirit teaches us of His love for us. - Matthew 11:28-30

God

Loves

You

Our ability to receive His love increases as

our revelation of His love for us increases. - I John 4:9-10

When we know we are loved by God, we walk with Him.

Sin loses its ability to hold on to us - we know our value.

God is Love

John 3:16 (NASB)

"For God so loved the world,

that He gave His only begotten Son,

that whoever believes in Him shall not perish,

but have eternal life.

I John 4:16 (NASB)

We have come to know and have believed

the love which God has for us.

God is love,

and the one who abides in love

abides in God, and God abides in him.

Romans 5:8 (NKJV)

But God demonstrates His own love toward us,

in that while we were still sinners,

Christ died for us.

I John 4:19 (NASB)

We love, because He first loved us.

How do we come into a place of repentance?

We cannot change ourselves. We need a Savior.

We are transformed by the presence of the Holy Spirit in us.

We receive the Holy Spirit when we receive Jesus into our hearts.

We must then also receive His forgiveness, acceptance and love.

This positions us in a place of fellowship with God.

We can walk with Him only if we are in fellowship with Him.

Jesus came to restore our relationship with God.

In the beginning,

God walked and talked with Adam and Eve in the garden.

After man sinned and God came for fellowship,

Adam and Eve hid themselves from Him.

Genesis 3:8-11 (NKJV)

And they heard the sound of the Lord God

walking in the garden in the cool of the day,

and Adam and his wife hid themselves

from the presence of the Lord God

among the trees of the garden.

Then the Lord God called to Adam and said to him,

"Where are you?"

So he said, "I heard Your voice in the garden,

and I was afraid because I was naked;

and I hid myself."

And He said, "Who told you that you were naked?

Have you eaten from the tree of which

I commanded you that you should not eat?"

The covering of God's glory that had been on man
had been removed through the sin which had occurred.
Sin had now become part of our human nature.
We inherited this sinful nature
through our flesh when we were born.
That is why we must be born again.
<u>We are born again when we put our faith in Jesus</u>.

<u>I Peter 1:23</u> (NIV)
<u>For you have been born again,</u>
not of perishable seed, but of imperishable,
through the living and enduring word of God.

Our heavenly Father loves us.
The Holy Spirit gives us this understanding.
He enables us to receive His truth
as His truth must be received into our spirits.
We have His presence in us through His Holy Spirit.

<u>II Corinthians 6:16</u> (NASB)
...<u>For we are the temple of the living God</u>;
just as God said,
"I will dwell in them and walk among them;
And I will be their God, and they shall be My people.

<u>II Corinthians 6:18</u> (NASB)
"<u>And I will be a father to you,</u>
And you shall be sons and daughters to Me,"
Says the Lord Almighty.

Jesus was the final sacrifice – it is finished.

People who wonder if they are included

do not understand that it is complete.

Nothing can be added to it. It was perfect and final

for all mankind for all time, for sins once for all.

Acts 13:38-39 (NASB)
"Therefore let it be known to you, brethren,

that through Him

forgiveness of sins is proclaimed to you,

and through Him

everyone who believes is freed from all things,

from which you could not be freed

through the Law of Moses.

Condemnation is the opposite of salvation.

Jesus died to give us salvation.

Having low self-esteem is the opposite of humility.

Humility is the absence of pride.

Micah 6:8 (NKJV)
He has shown you, O man, what is good;

And what does the Lord require of you

But to do justly,

To love mercy,

And to walk humbly with your God?

We can walk humbly with our Lord when we realize

that our righteousness is because of what He has done

for us, not because we could earn or deserve it.

Repentance means to change our mind.

In Greek, 'repentance' is 'metanoia' or 'change mind.'
When our thinking changes, our behavior follows.

Ephesians 4:23-24 (NASB)
and that you be renewed in the spirit
of your mind, and put on the new self,
which in the likeness of God has been created
in righteousness and holiness of the truth.

I Corinthians 2:16 (NIV)
"For who has known the mind of the Lord
that he may instruct Him?"
But we have the mind of Christ.

Colossians 3:10 (NASB)
and have put on the new self who is being renewed
to a true knowledge according to the image
of the One who created him -

Fixing our hope on Jesus purifies us.

I John 3:2-3 (NKJV)
Beloved, now we are children of God;
and it has not yet been revealed what we shall be,
but we know that when He is revealed,
we shall be like Him, for we shall see Him as He is.
And everyone who has this hope in Him
purifies himself, just as He is pure.

How can I be saved?

Romans 10:9-10 (NASB)

that if you confess with your mouth Jesus as Lord, and

believe in your heart that God raised Him from the dead,

you will be saved; for

with the heart a person believes, resulting in righteousness,

and with the mouth he confesses, resulting in salvation.

Acts 10:43 (NASB)

"Of Him all the prophets bear witness that

through His name everyone who believes in Him

receives forgiveness of sins."

Romans 5:1 (NIV)

Therefore, since we have been justified through faith,

we have peace with God through our Lord Jesus Christ,

Romans 8:1 (NIV)

Therefore, there is now no condemnation

for those who are in Christ Jesus,

<u>Receive Christ the Savior</u>
<u>A prayer of salvation</u>

Jesus - Forgive me of my sins.

You are the only begotten Son of God.

You lived a sinless life to be sacrificed for my redemption.

Your death on the cross fulfilled the payment for my sins.

You rose from the dead in righteousness

<u>for my justification</u>.

Only through what you have done am I made righteous.

I invite you to come into my heart.

I receive you as my Lord and Savior.

I place my life into your hands.

I love you as I receive your love for me.

I am forgiven. I am born again. I am a new creation.

I will follow You all the days of my life.

I have a future with you which extends into all eternity.

Thank You for loving me and ransoming me,

even while I was helpless.

Guide me in my life to be a witness of Your love.

We are sealed in the Holy Spirit <u>once we believe in our hearts</u>

<u>that Jesus is the only begotten Son of God</u>, that He was crucified

for our sins and rose again on the third day for our justification.

Only through the Holy Spirit can we receive this understanding

and that it applies to us personally. - Ephesians 1:13, 3:16-19, 4:30

John 14:15-17, 26, I John 2:25, 3:24, 4:13-15, 5:11-13, I Corinthians 12:3

<u>God</u>

<u>Sealed</u>

<u>You</u>

No one can say that Jesus is Lord without the Holy Spirit.

I Corinthians 12:3 - God gave us the Holy Spirit as a pledge that

<u>we will be with Him through eternity</u>. - II Corinthians 1:22, 5:5

Once we believe, we affirm our salvation through baptism.

You are sealed

II Corinthians 1:22 (NASB)
who also sealed us
and gave us the Spirit in our hearts
as a pledge.

Ephesians 1:13 (NKJV)
In Him you also trusted,
after you heard the word of truth,
the gospel of your salvation;
in whom also, having believed,
you were sealed
with the Holy Spirit of promise,

Romans 8:11 (NKJV)
But if the Spirit of Him
who raised Jesus from the dead
dwells in you,
He who raised Christ Jesus from the dead
will also give life to your mortal bodies
through His Spirit who dwells in you.

Eternal life is not temporary. - John 10:27-30

We are a spirit; we have a soul and we live in a body.

<u>Our spirit is joined with Christ once we receive Him as our Savior.</u>

His Spirit lives in us. His Spirit remains with us. - I Corinthians 6:17

He will never leave us nor forsake us. - Hebrews 13:5

<u>Our righteousness is in Him. - He saved us</u>. -Titus 3:4-6

<u>God</u>

<u>Assures</u>

<u>You</u>

Our faith is in Christ Jesus, not ourselves.

He is the Savior; He saves us from an eternity without Him.

Without Christ, we are lost to an eternity in hell.

<u>He sacrificed Himself to have us with Him - how great a love.</u>

That you know

I John 5:13 (NASB)
These things I have written to you
who believe in the name of the Son of God, so
that you may know that you have eternal life.

John 3:18 (NASB)
"He who believes in Him is not judged;
he who does not believe has been judged already,
because he has not believed in
the name of the only begotten Son of God.

I John 4:15 (NKJV)
Whoever confessed that Jesus is the Son of God,
God abides in him, and he in God.

John 6:40 (NASB)
"For this is the will of my Father, that everyone
who beholds the Son and believes in Him
will have eternal life, and
I Myself will raise him up on the last day."

Jesus said that he who believes in Him, 'From his
innermost being will flow rivers of living water.' - John 7:38-39

After Jesus was resurrected from the dead,
He breathed on His disciples and said, - John 20:22
"Receive the Holy Spirit."

He later told them to stay in Jerusalem - Acts 1:4-8
until the promise of the Holy Spirit had been given.
He told them to wait there until they were baptized
(totally immersed) in the Holy Spirit; - Acts 1:5
then they would receive power to be His witnesses.

The promise had not been given because
He had not yet been glorified. - John 7:39, 15:26, 16:7, 17:5
Jesus ascended into heaven, He was seated
at the right hand of the Father and received from
the Father the promise of the Holy Spirit. - Acts 2:32-33

He poured forth the Holy Spirit on the day of Pentecost.
This is what the prophet Joel foretold, that in the last days,
God would pour forth His Spirit on all mankind.
Acts 2:17-21, Joel 2:28-31

The Holy Spirit dwells in us once we believe in Jesus. - Ephesians 1:13
We are temples of the Holy Spirit. - I Corinthians 6:19, II Corinthians 6:16
Those who were immersed in the Holy Spirit on the
day of Pentecost, were then filled with Him again and again.
Although He remains with us once we believe,
He fills us as we stand as His witnesses.
Acts 4:8, 4:31, 6:8, 7:55, 8:17, 11:24, 13:9, 13:52

Later, the Holy Spirit fell upon those who
heard Peter proclaim that forgiveness of sins
is for <u>everyone who believes in Jesus</u>. - Acts 10:43

The Jews who were present saw that the Holy Spirit
had been given to the Gentiles (non-Jews) as well.
Acts 10:43-48, 11:15-17, Ephesians 4:4-6

They understood that they could not refuse to also

baptize them in water because the same Holy Spirit
which they had received, had also fallen upon them.

<u>There is only one Holy Spirit for us all</u>. - I Corinthians 12:13

The Holy Spirt is also for those who would believe
in Jesus in the future. - John 17:20, Acts 2:39

<u>Jesus said that we must be born again</u>. - <u>John 3:3-8</u>

He explains that we must be born of water and the Spirit.
In this same context, Jesus then explains what He means:
He tells us that which is born of the flesh is flesh (water)
and that which is born of the Spirit is spirit. (Spirit)

We have already been born of the flesh.
<u>We are born of the Spirit when we call on Jesus,</u>
<u>and believe in Him to receive Him into our hearts</u>.

<u>Jesus is the only begotten Son of God</u>.
When we believe in Jesus, God sends forth the Spirit
of His Son into our hearts, crying, "Abba! Father!"
We become adopted as children of God. – Galatians 4:5-6
The Lord is the Spirit. - II Corinthians 3:17
Jesus dwells in our hearts through faith. - Ephesians 3:17

Water baptism is the profession of our faith that
God wants and expects from each of us once we believe.
We are baptized into Christ Jesus. - Romans 6:3, Galatians 3:27
Baptism is affirming of our salvation.

In baptism, we express that we are one with the Lord:
We have died to ourselves as crucified with Him, being
buried with Him and are raised to live a new life in Him.
Colossians 3:3-4, Galatians 2:20-21, Romans 6:3-8

Baptism is a joyous occasion of resolve and assurance!

In baptism we are resolved to walk with Christ in new life.
If we are not willing to be baptized, we have not yielded
to the Lord for all that He has for us to walk in Him.

To say one is a Christian but not be baptized -
is to have a wedding and then miss saying, the "I do."
We cannot deny our Lord. It is never too late to be
baptized and even set an example to do so for others.

If a person is prevented from the opportunity of baptism upon
believing before they die, our Heavenly Father still receives them.
He knows our heart. We receive the Holy Spirit once we believe;
however, we should be baptized at first opportunity.
The first believers were baptized immediately.
Acts 8:36-39, 9:17-18, 10:43-48, 16:14-15, 16:30-34, 18:8, 19:4-5

God will often make a way for some in difficult situations
to be baptized even though it may not align with the more
conventional patterns that the traditions of the church have
accustomed us to. Review the above from the book of Acts.

What is baptism?

We are baptized into Christ Jesus -

having become united with Him in the likeness

of His death, burial and resurrection

to live to God in Him.

Romans 6:11, Matthew 28:19, Colossians 2:12-13

Romans 6:3-4 (NASB)

Or do you not know that all of us who have been baptized

into Christ Jesus have been baptized into His death?

Therefore we have been buried with Him through baptism

into death, so that as Christ was raised from the dead through

the glory of the Father, so we too might walk in newness of life.

Galatians 2:20 (NASB)

"I have been crucified with Christ; and it is no longer I who live,

but Christ lives in me; and the live which I now live in the flesh

I live by faith in the Son of God,

who loved me and gave Himself up for me.

Matthew 28:18-19 (NIV)

Then Jesus came to them and said,

"All authority in heaven and on earth has been given to me.

Therefore go and make disciples of all nations,

baptizing them in the name of

the Father and of the Son and of the Holy Spirit,

The Lord our God is one Lord

the Father - the Son - the Holy Spirit

Mark 12:29, Deuteronomy 6:4, Matthew 28:19

Jesus said, "I and the Father are one."- John 10:30

God said, "Let Us make man in Our image." - Genesis 1:26

God created man in His own image. - Genesis 1:27, 5:2

John 1:1, 1:3, (NASB)

In the beginning was the Word, and the Word was with God,
and the Word was God.

All things came into being through Him, and apart from Him
nothing came into being that has come into being.

The Word became flesh and dwelt among us, - I John 1:14
Jesus is the only begotten from the Father.

He has always existed. He has no beginning and no end.

Hebrews 1:2, 1:10, 2:10, Micah 5:2

Colossians 1:16-18 (NASB)

For by Him all things were created,

both in the heavens and on earth, visible and invisible,
whether thrones or dominions or
rulers or authorities – all things
have been created through Him and for Him.

He is before all things, and
in Him all things hold together.

He is also head of the body, the church; and
He is the beginning, the firstborn from the dead,...

The Father refers to His Son as God.

Hebrews 1:8-10 (NKJV) - Psalm 45:6-7

But to the Son He says:

"Your throne, O God, is forever and ever;

A scepter of righteousness is the scepter of Your kingdom.

You have loved righteousness and hated lawlessness;

Therefore God, Your God, has anointed You

With the oil of gladness more than Your companions."

And: "You, Lord,

in the beginning laid the foundation of the earth,

And the heavens are the work of Your hands.

Isaiah 42:5, 44:24, 48:13

Hebrews 1:2 (NIV)

but in these last days he has spoken to us by his Son,

whom he appointed heir of all things,

and through whom he made the universe.

Titus 2:13 (NASB)

looking for the blessed hope and the appearing

of the glory of our great God and Savior, Christ Jesus,

II Peter 1:1 (NASB)

Simon Peter, a bond-servant and apostle of Jesus Christ,

To those who have received a faith of the same kind as ours,

by the righteousness of our God and Savior, Jesus Christ:

Jesus has always existed

Micah 5:2 (NASB)

"But as for you, Bethlehem Ephrathah,
Too little to be among the clans of Judah, From you
One will go forth for Me to be ruler in Israel.
His goings forth are from long ago,
From the days of eternity."

Jesus left His place in glory

for a little while

Isaiah 9:6 (NKJV)

For unto us a Child is born, Unto us a Son is given;
And the government will be upon His shoulder.
And His name will be called Wonderful, Counselor,
Mighty God, Everlasting Father, Prince of Peace.

Mathew 1:23 (NKJV)

"Behold, the virgin shall be with child, and bear
a Son, and they shall call His name Immanuel,"
which is translated,
"God with us."

Hebrews 1:6 (NASB)

And when He again brings the firstborn into the world,
He says, "And let all the angels of God worship Him."

Jesus exists in the form of God

and yet - only for a little while

He was made as lower than the angels and
found in appearance as a man.
Hebrews 2:7-10, Psalm 8:5-6, Philippians 2:8

Philippians 2:6-7 (NASB)
who, although He existed in the form of God,

did not regard equality with God a thing to be grasped,

but emptied Himself, taking the form of a bond-servant,

and being made in the likeness of men.

Colossians 2:9 (NASB)
For in Him all the fullness of Deity dwells in bodily form,

God spent His own blood to redeem His church. - Acts 20:28
Only God could have borne the sins of the whole world.

Jesus is the only begotten of the Father.
We become adopted as children of God
Through faith in Christ Jesus.
John 1:14, Galatians 4:5, Ephesians 1:5

Galatians 4:6 (NASB)
Because you are sons, God has sent forth the Spirit
of His Son into our hearts, crying, "Abba! Father!"

II Corinthians 3:17 (NKJV)
Now the Lord is the Spirit; and
where the Spirit of the Lord is, there is liberty.

Jesus reigns with the Father

John 14:9 - whoever has seen Jesus has seen the Father.

John 20:28 -Thomas answered Jesus, "My Lord and my God!"

John 9:38 -The man born blind worshiped Him.

John 8:58 - Jesus said, "...before Abraham was born, I am."

John 5:18, 10:33 - He spoke as though equal with God.

Matthew 2:11 - The wise men worshiped Him.

Jesus left heaven and became a man.

He was for a little while lower than the angels.

He took our punishment that we could never bear.

He was crucified for our sins.

He conquered death and rose from the dead.

He is seated at the right hand of the Father.

He makes intercession for us. - Hebrews 7:25

He is glorified with the Father

as before the world began. -John 17:5,
Micah 5:2, Isaiah 9:6, 44:6

Acts 7:59 - Stephen yielded his spirit to Jesus upon death.

Philippians 2:6 - Jesus existed in the form of God.

Matthew 28:9 - the women at the tomb worshiped Him.

Mark 2:5-7, Luke 5:20-21 - He forgave sins, only God can forgive sins.

Matthew 14: 33, 28:17, Luke 24:52 - The disciples worshiped Him.

Revelation 1:17, 2:8, 22:13, Isaiah 48:12-13 - Jesus is the First and the Last.

Isaiah 44:6 - Only God is the First and the Last.

John 17:5 (NKJV)
"And now, O Father, glorify Me together with Yourself,
with the glory which I had with You before the world was.

Revelation 5:13 (NASB)
And every created thing which is in heaven and on the earth
and under the earth and on the sea, and all things in them,
I heard saying,
"To Him who sits on the throne, and to the Lamb,
be blessing and honor and glory
and dominion forever and ever."

Revelation 21:22 (NKJV)
But I saw no temple in it,
for the Lord God Almighty and the Lamb
are its temple.

Revelation 22:3, 22:5 (NASB)
There will no longer be any curse; and
the throne of God and of the Lamb will be in it,
and His bondservants will serve Him;
And there will no longer be any night;
and they will not have need of the light of a lamp
nor the light of the sun,
because the Lord God will illumine them;
and they will reign forever and ever.

Jesus endured the cross with us in view

Hebrews 12:2 (NKJV)
looking unto Jesus, the author and finisher of our faith,
who for the joy that was set before Him
endured the cross, despising the shame, and
has sat down at the right hand of the throne of God.

We are the joy that was set before Him.
He endured the cross to have us with Him.
He is seated at the right hand of the Father.
We are seated with Him. - Ephesians 2:6
We are one spirit with Him. - I Corinthians 6:17

Ephesians 2:6 (NASB)
and raised us up with Him, and seated us with Him
in the heavenly places in Christ Jesus,

I Corinthians 6:17 (NASB)
But the one who joins himself to the Lord
is one spirit with Him.

We join ourselves to the Lord when we trust Him
as our Savior. He wants us with Him. - John 17:24, 14:3, 12:26
Jesus died to redeem us to Himself. - Titus 2:14
Through our redemption in Christ,
we receive love, forgiveness and acceptance.

God designed us in His own image.

We are designed for Him to dwell in us.

Fellowship with our heavenly Father is about prayer.

It is being aware of His presence with us.

It is being guided by His Holy Spirit in us.

It is understanding our value to Him.

Romans 8:32, Ephesians 1:17-19

His thoughts are continually on us. - Psalm 40:5, 139:17-19

He knows the number of hairs on our head. - Matthew 10:30

He has prepared a place for us so that we will be with Him.

He will return and receive us to Himself. - John 14:3

We have an eternal future abiding in His love and glory.

Revelation 21:3-5 (NASB)

And I heard a loud voice from the throne, saying,

"Behold, the tabernacle of God is among men, and

He will dwell among them, and they shall be His people,

and God Himself will be among them, and

He will wipe away every tear from their eyes;

and there will no longer be any death; there will

no longer be any mourning, or crying, or pain;

the first things have passed away."

And He who sits on the throne said,

"Behold, I am making all things new."

And He said,

"Write, for these words are faithful and true."

Those who believe

II Corinthians 5:17 (NKJV)

Therefore, if anyone is in Christ,

he is a new creation;

old things have passed away;

behold, all things have become new.

I John 3:1 (NASB)

See how great a love

the Father has bestowed on us,
that we would be called

children of God;

and such we are. For this reason
the world does not know us,

because it did not know Him.

I Corinthians 2:12 (NKJV)

Now we have received,

not the spirit of the world, but

the Spirit who is from God,

that we may know the things that

have been freely given to us by God.

God is for us

Romans 8:31-34 (NASB)

What then shall we say to these things?

If God is for us,

who is against us?

He who did not spare His own Son,

but delivered Him over for us all,

how will He not also with Him

freely give us all things?

Who will bring a charge against God's elect?

God is the one who justifies;

who is the one who condemns?

Christ Jesus is He who died,

yes, rather who was raised,

who is at the right hand of God,

who also intercedes for us.

Romans 2:4 (NIV)

Or do you show contempt for the riches

of His kindness, tolerance and patience,

not realizing that God's kindness

leads you toward repentance?

Receive Jesus & abide in Him

Jesus will say to some, "I never knew you."
Matthew 7:21-23, 25:12, Luke 13:26-27, John 16:3, 1 John 2:19

They did works in His name, but they never received Him.

They did not receive Him into their hearts as their Lord.

They never walked with Him. – Colossians 1:27, 2:6-10

God created us for fellowship with Him. – Ephesians 3:17

He gave us the choice to receive or reject Him.

Love is an act of free will.

He wants to be truly loved by us.

Every person wants to be loved

because we are made in His image.

God is love.

Realizing the love God has for us

is to receive His love.

He wants us to know Him.

He wants us to be known by Him.
I Corinthians 8:3, Galatians 4:9

He wants us to receive His love and love Him in return -

to believe in Him, trust Him and walk with Him. – John 17:3

He wants to say to us, "Well done good and faithful servant."

We are a friend to Jesus if we love one another. – John 15:12-15

Those who do the will of the Father are His family.

Matthew 25:23, 12:50, Mark 3:35, Luke 8:21, 11:27-28, John 13:34-35

Ephesians 3:17 (NKJV)

that Christ may dwell in your hearts through faith;

that you, being rooted and grounded in love,

Ephesians 3:19 (NASB)

and to know the love of Christ

which surpasses knowledge, that you may be

filled up to all the fullness of God.

Luke 10:27 (NASB) Matthew 22:37-39, Mark 12:29-31

And he answered, "You shall love the Lord your God

with all your heart, and with all your soul,

and with all your strength, and with all your mind;

and your neighbor as yourself."

I Corinthians 8:3 (NASB)

but if anyone loves God, he is known by Him.

Colossians 2:6 (NASB)

Therefore as you have received

Christ Jesus the Lord, so walk in Him,

I John 4:9 (NKJV)

In this the love of God was manifested toward us,

that God has sent His only begotten Son into the world,

that we might live through Him.

Jesus is the Shepherd

Christ reveals Himself in Scripture for us to know Him.

Once His word is received into our spirits,

we have a recognition of who He really is. - John 10:3-4

If something does not line up with His word,

we know it is not from Him. - John 10:5

We know Him and He knows His own. - John 10:14-15

Jesus is the good Shepherd. - John 10:11

He lays down His life for His sheep.

A shepherd leads his sheep so they will follow him.

Hearing His voice, His Spirit in us, guides us to follow Him.

Following Jesus is true repentance. - Psalm 23

His sheep hear His voice and follow Him. - John 10:27-30

and follow Him.

and follow Him.

He came to feed the sheep, not beat the sheep. - Jeremiah 3:15

Jesus rejoices over finding a lost sheep! - Luke 15:1-7, 19:10

A shepherd is to feed the sheep, strengthen the sickly,

heal the diseased, bind up the broken and seek the lost.

Ezekiel 34;1-5 - Jesus came for this reason. - Matthew 9:35-36

The kindness of God leads us to repentance. - Romans 2:4

He is the Shepherd and Guardian of our souls. - I Peter 2:24-25

Jesus appoints shepherds who love Him. - John 21:15-17

Others who dominate, scatter the sheep. - Ezekiel 34:4

Having been justified by faith, we have peace with God.

We can know that He is pleased to have us follow Him.

Isaiah 40:11 (NASB)

Like a shepherd He will tend His flock,

In His arm He will gather the lambs

And carry them in His bosom;

He will gently lead the nursing ewes.

Jeremiah 3:15 (NKJV)

"And I will give you shepherds according to My heart,

who will feed you with knowledge and understanding.

Psalm 23:3 (NKJV)

He restores my soul;

He leads me in the paths of righteousness

For His name's sake.

John 12:26 (NKJV)

"If anyone serves Me, let him follow Me;

and where I am, there My servant will be also.

If anyone serves Me, him My Father will honor.

Matthew 11:28-30 (NASB)

"Come to Me, all who are weary and heavy-laden,

and I will give you rest.

"Take My yoke upon you and learn from Me,

for I am gentle and humble in heart,

and you will find rest for your souls.

"For My yoke is easy and My burden is light."

Jesus is the Vine

When we abide in Christ's love, we keep His commandments.
His commandment is that we love one another. - John 15:10-12
If we abide in Him, we walk as He walks. - I John 2:6, Colossians 2:6

In Christ, we have bold access to the Father through prayer.
If we ask anything in Jesus name, the Father answers. - John 16:23
'In Jesus name' means on His behalf, according to His will.

Jesus is the vine. We are the branches. - John 15:5
Apart from Him, we can do nothing.

can do nothing.

can do nothing.

If we put our focus on fellowship with Him,
He will complete all that He desires to do in our lives.
By this we will become all that He has created us to be.

Jesus lived the perfect example of fellowship with God.
He finished all the Father sent Him to do. - John 17:4, 19:30
Jesus did only what He saw His Father doing. - John 5:19, 12:50

We do His work through fellowship with Him. - John 15:4-5
He wants us to do away with dead works. - Hebrews 9:14
His work has eternal results. - Luke 10:42, Matthew 6:20

Jesus shared the Father's glory before the world was. - John 17:5
We glorify the Father when we bear fruit through Him. - John 15:8

When we believe in Jesus, He works through us. - John 6:29
This is the fellowship that God wants us to experience with Him.

Ephesians 2:10 (NKJV)

For we are His workmanship,

created in Christ Jesus for good works,

which God prepared beforehand

that we should walk in them.

I Corinthians 2:9 (NKJV)

But as it is written:

"Eye has not seen, nor ear heard,

Nor have entered into the heart of man

The things which God has prepared

for those who love Him."

Jeremiah 29:11 (NASB)

'For I know the plans that I have for you,'

declares the Lord, 'plans for welfare and

not for calamity to give you a future and a hope.

Philippians 1:6 (NASB)

For I am confident of this very thing, that

He who began a good work in you will perfect it

until the day of Christ Jesus.

Ephesians 3:20 (NKJV)

Now to Him who is able to do exceedingly

abundantly above all that we ask or think,

according to the power that works in us.

Jesus is the Word

<u>Jesus came as God's word in the flesh</u>. - John 1:14

His life on earth displayed His love for us.

He healed and delivered all who came to Him. - Matthew 12-15

<u>Jesus never refused anyone because of their sin</u>. - I Timothy 1:15

He came to release us from our sins. - Matthew 1:21, Acts 13:38-39

He made us clean by the word which He spoke to us. - John 15:3

<u>Jesus is the Word of God</u>. - Revelation 19:13

Meditation on God's word brings His truth into our spirits.

We need this understanding for the Holy Spirit to transform us.

<u>God's word in us is eternal – His Word is Christ in us</u>.

His presence in us, through His Holy Spirit, manifests

His love to us. We should manifest His love

to others through His Holy Spirit in us.

Scripture is the foundation for every Christian to stand upon.

Scripture is solid who we are in relation to our Heavenly Father.

<u>He claims us as His. In Christ, we are righteous before God</u>.

Scripture gives understanding for assurance of our salvation.

<u>Jesus paid the penalty for our sins</u>.

We who are in Christ are not judged.

<u>We are in Christ once we believe in Him</u>.

We have passed from death into life. - John 5:24

God wants us to receive the love He has for us and come boldly

before Him with assurance of our righteousness in Him.

<u>It is through this fellowship with Him that we are transformed</u>.

John 1:1-3 (NASB)

In the beginning was the Word, and the Word
was with God, and the Word was God.

He was in the beginning with God.
All things came into being through Him,
and apart from Him nothing
came into being that has come into being.

John 1:14 (NKJV)

And the Word became flesh
and dwelt among us, and we beheld His glory,
the glory as of the only begotten of the Father,
full of grace and truth.

Hebrews 4:12 (NASB)

For the word of God is living and active
and sharper than any two-edged sword, and piercing as far
as the division of soul and spirit, of both joints and marrow,
and able to judge the thoughts and intentions of the heart.

Matthew 24:35, Mark 13:31, Luke 21:33 (NASB)

"Heaven and earth will pass away,
but My words will not pass away.

John 5:24 (NKJV)

"Most assuredly, I say to you, he who hears My word
and believes in Him who sent Me has everlasting life,
and does not come into judgement,
but has passed from death into life.

The Old Testament / The New Testament

The Old Testament tells of creation until the time of Christ.

The New Testament tells of Christ through the end of Revelation.

In the New Testament, Old Testament covenants are fulfilled

with the final covenant of redemption through Christ Jesus.

The final covenant is between the Father and the Son -

Jesus is our High Priest forever - it is eternal.
Hebrews 7:24-28, 9:11-14, 13:20-21

The Old Testament is the New Testament concealed.

The New Testament is the Old Testament revealed.

This brings validity to both as neither could have

happened as the other was written without a divine plan.

It is amazing that we live in a time to actually have
the Old Testament and the New Testament of the Bible
completed, displayed before us and at our access.
The Old Testament proves the New Testament as it foreshadows

it with its prophets, prototypes and displays of God's providence.

The Bible has been proven as its prophecies have been fulfilled

with the unfolding of history throughout thousands of years.

We need to read and receive the Bible on our own.

It should be part of our daily conversation with God.

Jesus is revealed throughout all of Scripture. - Luke 24:27, 44-47

His word is for each of us – His word in us is eternal.

God wants us to receive His Word into our hearts.

His Holy Spirit reveals His Word to us as we read it.

The Holy Spirit anoints us with understanding to

receive that which is Spirit and truth - His truth. - John 17:17

Taking scripture out of context can change its meaning.

It is important to read scriptures before and after a scripture

in order to know the context from which it was taken.

The meaning can be completely different if not in context.

It is important to know to whom the scripture was written,

to those who are in Christ or to those who do not know Him.

It is important to know when the scripture was written,

to know which covenant those receiving it were under.

Jesus came to give us life and give it abundantly. - John 10:10

Relationship with Him is one of love, confidence and joy.

In Him, we are forgiven, accepted and favored.

God disciplines us to train us unto life not destruction.

In Him we have been redeemed from the curse of the Law.

Galatians 3:13 - Our punishment has been paid.

Not everything written before the resurrection of Christ

is to be practiced by us now or is still required of us today.

It is read for our understanding in the telling of His story,

it is our story about our Creator who loves us so dearly.

He wants us to know Him and our value to Him.

As we know His love for us, we walk in fellowship with Him.

We become Christ-like in our character.

The Holy Spirit remains with us

God said, - Hosea 4:6

"My people perish for lack of knowledge,"

But

The time would come, God said, when Shepherds after

His own heart – Jeremiah 3:15

will feed His sheep on knowledge and understanding.

Once basic truths are established in a person's heart,

they cannot be taken away.

Jesus said no one can take His sheep from His hand.

His sheep hear His voice and He knows them.

They follow Him. - John 10:27

In the Old Testament, the Holy Spirit would come upon a person

but He would not stay. Now that we have been redeemed by

the blood of Jesus Christ, we have taken on His righteousness.

He sent the Holy Spirit to remain with us forever.

The Holy Spirit leads us to believe in Jesus.

Once we believe in Christ, we are one spirit with Him.

He will never leave us nor forsake us.

I Corinthians 6:17, Hebrews 13:5

John 14:16 (NASB)

"I will ask the Father, and He will give you

another Helper, that He may be with you forever;

Matthew 28:20 (NASB)

… I am with you always, even to the end of the age."

Hebrews 13:5 (NKJV)

…I will never leave you nor forsake you,"

John 10:28 (NASB)

and I give eternal life to them,

and they will never perish;

and no one will snatch them out of My hand.

Jeremiah 31:3 (NASB)

…I have loved you with an everlasting love;

Therefore I have drawn you with lovingkindness.

Our Spiritual warfare

In Christ, we have bold access to the Father through prayer.

He has though given us authority to bind spirits in His name.

We can also release the power of the Holy Spirit.

<u>Our warfare is not against flesh and blood</u>. - Ephesians 6:12

Our warfare is against unbelief, deception, pride...

We must recognize spiritual influences everyday as

we encounter people, situations and circumstances.

We respond differently knowing that it is a testing for us.

<u>These influences oppose the Spirit of Christ in us</u>.

We must remember that we represent Him

in everything that we say and do. - II Corinthians 10:3-6

<u>If we stay in agreement with the Spirit of Christ</u>,

we do not respond in the same spirit which is attacking us.

This is our victory over these opposing influences.

Greater is He who is in us than He who is in the world.

This is truly the fellowship that Jesus wants with us.

<u>Obedience to Him demonstrates our alliance with Him</u>.

This is Love. He is our protector, provider and friend.

He is God and He created us in His own image.

In Christ, we are righteous before God.

In Christ, we belong to Him. - I John 4:13-15, 3:24

<u>We overcome wrong influences by knowing we are His</u>.

We have victory through the blood of the Lamb

and the word of our testimony. - Revelation 12:11

Made in the USA
Columbia, SC
04 August 2024

39988103R00035